STANDING WATER

Standing Water

ELEANOR CHAI

FARRAR STRAUS GIROUX

NEW YORK

Farrar, Straus and Giroux
18 West 18th Street, New York 10011

Grateful acknowledgment is made for permission to reprint the following material:
Pages 8–9: From *The Metamorphoses* by Ovid, translated by Horace Gregory,
translation copyright © 1958 by The Viking Press, Inc.; copyright renewed ©
1986 by Patrick Bolton Gregory. Used by permission of Viking Books, an imprint
of Penguin Publishing Group, a division of Penguin Random House LLC.
Page 15: Masque de Hanako, type E, photograph copyright © Musée Rodin
(photo: Christian Baraja). Pages 34–36: Lines adapted from a passage in Loie Fuller's
Fifteen Years of a Dancer's Life that was quoted in Donald Keene's *Appreciations of
Japanese Culture*. Used by kind permission of Donald Keen. Page 41: Masque de Hanako,
type D, variante, photograph copyright © Musée Rodin (photo: Pauline Hisbacq).

Library of Congress Cataloging-in-Publication Data
Names: Chai, Eleanor, 1967–
Title: Standing water : poems / Eleanor Chai.
Description: New York: Farrar, Straus and Giroux, 2016.
Identifiers: LCCN 2015035372 | ISBN 9780374269487 (hardback) |
ISBN 9780374714918 (e-book)
Subjects: | BISAC: POETRY / American / Asian American.
Classification: LCC PS3603.H3348 A6 2016 | DDC 811/.6—dc23
LC record available at http://lccn.loc.gov/2015035372

Our books may be purchased in bulk for promotional, educational, or
business use. Please contact your local bookseller or the Macmillan Corporate
and Premium Sales Department at 1-800-221-7945, extension 5442,
or by e-mail at MacmillanSpecialMarkets@macmillan.com.

www.fsgbooks.com
www.twitter.com/fsgbooks
www.facebook.com/fsgbooks

1 3 5 7 9 10 8 6 4 2

DEDICATION

Everything I am is
Us. Come home.

GEORGE OPPEN

Contents

Opticks

This is her descending
glance captured
in a hidden photograph

taken when I was
an infant and Mother held me
at arm's length. I look back

for her, unsurprised
still questioning why she doesn't return
my gaze. Her eyes

fix on a spot between
her face and my face. For the infant
there is no distinction.

Her disaffection stains the intimate
objects found years later
among her things of everyday:

a thimble embroidered with a single petal.
A slim gold watch—stopped.
Brushes held to

dry in a bamboo roll. A tiny lime
and fuchsia dress sewn by her
hands for my hundredth day.

His wedding band, scarred
a muted gray. In the gap between us
a vacancy swells and bellies

the air where her eyes avert mine
to slide off where? I wish I could see her
engage and ignite

these traces of the ordinary,
the minutely particular
totems of our daily life: *holy*.

In an old dream, I plot a little boy's flight.
Like a fighter pilot, I drop
a homing device back in time to spy

into the landscape of my infancy
before she turned her face away—
before my need was extraordinary.

Mare

FOR ETP

Standing in a small January rain
I look into the wet convex
surface of the horse's tired gaze.

I will not push myself in—
I wait for the giant muzzle to inch
nearer to my darkened eyes: wide

open. I wait for something
I cannot guess will arrive.
I hush as I wait. I tell myself

the smell of horse may be
as close as I will come to what
I seek. The beast begins

to feel safe.

*

Before she was taken, she was playing
outside with friends looking for flowers,
running from (or following) snakes.

They were by a lake.

> In the myth,
> that the lake was bordered by trees bearing thick
> foliage, that the ground around the lake was shaded,
> seems important to the tale.
> Its botanical situation is always mentioned:
> a body of water surrounded by a bower
> is where she was designated to play.
> Winnicott might call this her "potential space."

*

Past the cool shade of trees
orbiting the water, he saw her step into the sun.
He felt a need take him. In a blur for both

he was on her, in her, above and over her.
It was just the beginning— She couldn't close her eyes
to blot out the tattoos inking his arms

as he pushed through her. Snow-capped
mountains with clouds drifting by.
A valley emptying into the sea. A small

fishing boat. A fisherman in coolie pants grinning
or grimacing, she couldn't tell which.
On the other arm, a field of wheat,

a few specks of birds, oxen, two fat women,
flowers strewn in the summery scene.
Then it was done. He gathered her close.

She didn't resist. He rocked her a little.
He whistled for his horses. They cantered forth, not far
from the sounds of her friends, still playing by the lake.

He inserted himself into her that day.
He will always be where she is.
He will live a life within her.

She will never live a day alone.

*

In the myth, he kidnapped her.
She doesn't know how long they rode. She knows
they stopped—she smelled the sea. They were at a bay named
for the nymph Cyane. It rippled in slow, smooth waves.

A woman was in the water, a woman of those waters.
She started to approach the two on horseback,
but the little girl's small, torn, dirt-stained dress, her dazed stare
stopped her. *She's someone's child.* Save her. She would try.

Cyane rose from those waters to fight. The man hissed,
"Don't try me, Nymph. I will tear you to bits.
I will ride a road through you," and he did.
He parted her, taking his child-bride underground.

This is not a scholarly footnote in Ovid: it is there
in Book Five of the *Metamorphoses*.
A slim nymph reified the heroic.

Unhealed,
        incurable and all in tears, she melted.
Her slimmest parts went first: hair, nails,

fingers, and feet. She swayed there dismembered—
        bald with no eyebrows, no eyelashes,
with fingerless hands and footless ankles.

Her hairless skull turned pellucid with her torso
         and her limbs, where one could see a small
stream system within the larger body of water:

her veins ran not with blood, but with clear water
         until even the inner membranes dissolved and
there was nothing to see, nothing to hold.

                                    *

Cyane was not defending what was hers,
not avenging a personal injury. In the face of a force
she could not perceive, she rose from her buoying
comfort to aid a child, save a child not of her making.

She lost everything she was and would be.
She came apart, melting—*Unhealed, incurable, dissolved.*
Left there strewn across the bay, *dismembered*
—forever, her inner membranes move

the surface of those waters—as light flecks and curves
the grape pulp of the swollen convex eye of the Mare I seek.
Those waters animate every such Beast. She looks
unflinchingly. I stand still, euphoric to be seen until I am

inside, yoked to the stream falling from her eyes, the harm
of those waters reflects the hunger and sorrow of the beast

lowering her head to me. She gives no sign.
She continues to watch. Her nostrils flare. She can smell no fear:

I am not afraid.
I've already been wounded.
That's not why I stay.

Unhealed, imperfect: she gives me her gaze,
surface into which I can *almost* vanish, *begin* to disappear
until, in the eye of a mare I begin to see *all I cannot let go*:
every cut, every thrust, each handle-less blade.

Where the skin has smoothed over, in her eye
I feel the white sting. My memory of it is visible
in the jelly of the horse's eye, the surface
skimming the waters of Cyane.

The beast nuzzles in.

*

In every purloined childhood, there lives a fantasy,
a Dreamed-of One who tries to heal the rift. Persephone
doesn't have to wish her, she's there. Ovid wrote her

into the myth. While Persephone lies in his Darkness,
an inlet of water rolls in her mind: a membrane of movement
sequined with light. Under such light there is life.

Raped, mutilated, and damaged: deep
inside it is possible she remains as pure as when she arrived—
her time was stopped by his seizure, her abduction.

*

From one body of water, we are given. I took
my nascence from one who was left behind.
There was no nymph to save us, no Cyane to try.

This is the cipher of my body— I leached the living
waters of the one who gave me. I took my leave
transfused with every infant need, I became

her one caul too many, the film that made living
unbearable. The life that followed
her insistence on my birth was her killing stick.

Little Hanako

In the first electric light, *Little Hanako*,
Maître Rodin's "tiny transvestite" drives
a blade into her kimono. Blood blooms.

Red wounds the synthetic white.
Masticating muscles and sockets rise
beneath her skin, casting a grimace performed

each night. Her ritually wide-open eyes show
her, dying—to return *alive*. The stage goes dim
with her vanishing. He is held

to his seat. She is a heavy dream.
She straps him down as if in sleep. Before he may rise,
she must sit—hold still—alone, for him.

Yeats's fan-dancer, Loie Fuller, arranges it . . .

"Attends, attends . . . pas beaucoup Hanako!"
He draws the spare distance to a few little hairs
at the bottom of her muscled torso—bare

squiggled strokes, "*et en dessous, ta petite fleur,*" quite closed.
From underneath, a pale abalone glow flutes across an inland sea.
It is the life beneath her sex he seeks.

Standing Water

1

A starless summer evening in Paris
after Garden paths, small Museums,

looking long at the bronze Kabuki actor
transvestite/tiny dancer: Rodin's Hanako

Head of Sorrow, where we stand
transfixed—stagnant, like standing water.

Nothing new was falling from the sky
—nothing flowing from far or

nearby—no human egg was there
fertilized, but the water standing for so long

a time teemed with spiral bacteria
Dragonfly nymphs, Mosquito larvae.

2

A finer incubator for plague than running or
flowing water, standing water poses

a grave danger when the weather is warm enough.
A breeding kingdom for vectors and disease lies

beneath the still impassive surface—
Malaria. Yellow-Fever. Cholera. Parasites

thrive, living off the living
to survive. They multiply and gain strength,

gain strength and multiply.
Strain

humanity will never be rid of—

3

After the setting sun, in a garden-
room of a restaurant with sinewy trees lit

by tiny lights, we read the menu and talk
about the glittering beauty of the city.

We look, each into the face of the other and see
no one there to see, but forms insinuating visions;

—absent faces in retreat. I sit sealed in reverie
(*close as skin*) as he becomes agitated, tight-jawed

still more chiseled: the stone of a god—

He pours my first glass of wine (after I decline) he fills it
half way to the lip, he nods Hard—(black)-eyes the glass
untouched. I sip in little swigs so he won't erupt.

Whatever he was looking for or from
I am the uninvited one.

4

Uninvited, I eat through a quiet

summer rain falling in slow paths through
a ritual (feral rite-of-passage) of five courses, splendidly set.

I eat only what I know, avoid the rest.
I chew through some one thing from each bone-white plate:
a garnish, lettuce leaves, edible flowers, slim green beans.

[19]

We adjourn to the lounge, he orders cognac (for one),
sits in a tufted chair to tell me, teach me

the primordial lines of design (mine). My
coming into being   by way of   *before-my-beginning*

in the sturdy smoke of cigars and squinting
men eyeing me from their watering-hole—O
            —pardon me: their *exotic-wood* bar.

5

A cloth-maker magnified
        a drop of standing rain,
            a drop long standing.

He named what he saw
        Little Animals in Rain Water (1702)

"In all falling rain,
        carried from gutters
            into water-butts,

and in all kinds of
　　water, standing
　　　　in the open air, animalcules

can turn up."

6

Everywhere I look
little animals turn up
a second swelling glance
the sudden rushing bloom to a head
the half-turned adjustment of a pants-leg—

("*et en dessous, ta petite fleur*," Maître Rodin said)

See, I have this new piece I walk with-
in this new body that brings
(*invites*) sniffing, eye-

balls—avid
yen for release,
mere release, no relief: nothing
spent, no debt, just an emptying out
to refill again—

like multiplying rats, like trash: collects
does not renew—waste the female
form does best without
can do without but without:

nothing new comes forth, is born.

7

He begins in quiet tones
like water, standing in open air,
trembles at ponderous movements
furrows on the surface from the wind.

The allegory begins
in a guilty desire *(not sin)*.
When my *Native Mother* was pregnant
with me, he intended to interrupt her pregnancy

Disrupt the *(my)* growth
to save her *(or them or us)*
from one more spell of postpartum
sadness-unto-savagery—

Someone will take my children from me.
Someone I know but cannot see. Who
will it be? They? Or you? Or he?
I? Or she? Or ME?

8

It was the Seventies. No, late Sixties—
the politic of the time stalled his design to avert her

final desolation, "She got so sick after the first two,
another would have finished her . . . What she wanted?

She wanted a girl. I would have forced her, but I couldn't.
Only one doctor agreed to it . . . in his living room."

Too poor to travel to more catholic surrounds, my birth
(*not beginning, you just heard my beginning and so did I*) was allowed.

Thus, in a warm, wet surround, I grew and
multiplied, and multiplying

I grew, came forth.

9

Viewed through a microscope, the bacterium *Vibrio cholerae*
                                                quivers or vibrates.

Alone, a single vibrator is harmless. Simple physical contact
                                                with the rotating

flagellum poses no threat. It needs to get inside to find its force:
                                                ingest the little creatures,

it launches its theatre. With a little help, a protein, it reproduces
                                                at full swift: a siege.

A population explosion within releases toxin into the cells lining
                                                the small intestines.

It disrupts a vital metabolic role: water balance, absorption of
                                                water and its passing

into the body proper. The secreting cells, once done, are
                                                released as waste.

V. cholerae disrupts the balance, reverses through deception.
                                                Cholera toxin tricks

the cells into expelling at a gross rate. The evacuated water is
                                    populated with flakes,

cells of the small intestine. White particles inspired the oriental,
                                    visual "rice water."

Death by dehydration derived from a simple organism found in
                                    warm standing water

is ingested into its own Elysium: the moist, warm loam of the bowel,
                                    forcing rapid secretion.

10

He continues. He goes for the kill.
I can see it in his eyes, I can feel it in mine:

they dilate wide as eggs.
I will not flinch at what he says.

"Once you were born, she was never the same,
but I didn't really know her anyway . . .
I met her once before we married.
With the boys, she was strange for a few months
. . . she got better. With you, she stayed *strange*" —

What does he mean by his *strange*—? Where she stayed?
—Why did he think it was there she'd remain?

Is it illness if her plaguing fears, then called *severe paranoia*
actually comes true and in months, in years, are memories?

Echolalia or chorus or recurrence: recurring into a future:
past—irretrievable (yes, it sounds like willed tragedy, a movie).

Symptoms of Dementia Praecox. Odd-job words:
container for no one term, terms that cannot be contained

words for which there is no one meaning, like *meaning*
so says Wittgenstein in *The Blue Book*—

OR is the danger real: present, always?

Still in the lounge, stretching it out as long as he can,
he pauses, sniffs from the bowl of the glass

                                  swirls, tips:

the amber barely moistens his lips. He looks at me as if
I'm a game of chess. Each shift, sip constitute

a move

a maneuver in a game I've never played. I don't know
the rules; I have no means to imagine strategies.

I want him

to finish his winning, let me still from all this spinning.
I'm dizzy, nauseous—but he is at my beginning,

so I sit. I stay.

He coils the ends of his reasoning into a spring: anger
at my estrangement in this new body almost removed

before it was made.

13

She who made me, made me in her likeness.
I was she before I was mine, or yours or his, or I.

My square head and Westerner's wide eyes were questioned
in regard to my worth and blessing.

My mother said my face was prophetic, meaning foretelling
or ominous, or both. Though it's possible she didn't know

what she saw or meant to see. Whatever I was to her,
she was relieved for me.—

Since I favored my paternal line, I might be spared
her queer hungers of mind (whatever they were or would be).

And both parents believed (through hope or hoax)
my fecund face would not drop her into the post-partum hole

she barely ascended after dropping two boys to the earth.

14

Needy double *(she/I)* showed her who she was, what
she really wanted—

She wanted to stay merged with her likeness, there
would be no others. She wanted to do as her creation did.

But all *I* did was suck and piss and shit into cloth and cry
and scream and shake and wake the world when it needed

rest, because that's what infants do.
She was neat as a pin, quiet as tea and as proud as she *could* be.

She got very still, as if she were balancing a jug of water on her head. She moved as little as possible, so she wouldn't get wet.

15

A flood released me, freed me to squirm
from harm but my legs, still furled, didn't

know how to run—so I lay in ivory arms,
her swollen lap: my first ground. There

I wait, legs splayed, never curled in alarm.
Learned to sleep through the burn of being

split like a trunk. In the tree of my body
the culm is flushed, dank and sharp. Sweet-

bitter the sap that was taken in the dark.

16

You owed this after the pain you caused
forcing abrupt separation, internment to far asylum

leaving him children to tend, except you, sent
to live in a far out of sight until your infant's face changed

into a small girl child who never knew the chain her
exhaustive gestation sent to strangle the whole of a young family.

Unwinding and lashing on that warm Paris night,
he wrapped these links—a demented pearl cuff

tight to her throat, shutting her up. She stared and bled
blue from her new shoes, a little more bloodless than he,

hardly surprised, as if she already knew.

17

I rely on fixed prohibitions. I lust for totems.
I do my best to eat them, to own them.

But I bow my head in reverence before true Taboos.
Ethnographers have discovered so few

Universals, when a rule from one tribe is obeyed across
deserts and forests and oceans

it would be hubris to scorn them or ignore them.
The taboo I cling to concerns

boundaries intact, unriven borders of skin.
Hidden openings;

no lacuna should be calved so
close to one's beginning.

18

Proscriptions were broken.
A father's self-betrayed: my mother's

descent into madness

upon my appearance was the context—
no, *the reason* improvised for my rape.

A numbness grew inside

out in the Firstborn. The last child
who sent their Mother away was returned

in her place.

The feminized face became, for this abandoned son,
an icon, a fetish—praxis of rage.

19

If I had kept silent, if I hadn't looked like I was always receding
from a hard blow to somewhere in my torso

my father promised he never would have told me about my fault
in the dark matter of the Firstborn whose first

six years were erased when his mother and her infant girl vanished.
The infant (I) reemerged as a young child

to watch from a distance perceived and hallowed in my mind.
This family haunted by a mother calling for her

Firstborn, eager echographer, devoted to carving a map of her
   noise-
less sounds into the last body she bled for, milked *(more?)*

to pin-point her exact location in the cartography of his grief-
   wracked mind.
A father, relying on the warmth of the last child

to leave un-etched the veneer labored to glaze like the black lacquer
    trays
we used for green tea and bean paste on birthdays.

20

What was it about seeing the *Head of Sorrow, Head of Hanako*,
after eating sorbet cones by the path from the pond?

Head of Little Flowers, how could you have caused
a father to speak so? You are where it began.

I can see us now, approaching your bust slowing our advance
dropping hands, parting, stopping

where we stand, neither of us looking into your eyes
both of us watching you, both of us

surprised by who we see. I wanted to turn away, and so
I think, did he, but we didn't.

We stood before you, each of us in our own orifice of standing water.

When she was heavy with me, she designed and dug
a small pond in the back of our house, empty now,
where rain water collects. When the weather is warm

enough, *Vibrio cholorae* form. If it's too cold there
then they form here, or anywhere, or everywhere
within us, around us, kept in check only by set numbers,

threat humanity will never be rid of.
That blue-lipped death wants only human lips to color.
Beneath the stars or starless nights that fix or falsify

our fate, it waits: telluric.

Loie Fuller, Yeats's fan-dancer, describing Little Hanako's suicide
in the Kabuki performance that transfixed Rodin, wrote:

With little movements
like those of a frightened

child, with sighs with cries
as of a wounded

bird, she rolled herself
into a ball

to reduce her thin body to
a mere nothing

it was lost
in the fold

of her embroidered robe.
Her face became

immoveable, as if
petrified, her eyes

continued
to reveal intense animation . . .

Some little hiccoughs convulsed her:
she made a little outcry

and then another so faint
it was hardly more than a sigh.

Finally, with great wide-open eyes
she surveyed death which had just overtaken her.

Thrilling.

23

—and I am back, in that crimson velvet chair
beneath a watery ceiling by Chagall and a vast crystal chandelier.

I can't take my eyes from the stage where Iphigénie sings her heart
    away.

I can't hear the difference between *cours* and *coeur*, so when she begs,
Stop this rage, this suffering, this war—I hear: *I beg of you, Stop this*
    heart:

(I wish to die, I implore)
                    —I hear *her* vibrato again trilling
in my ear, I know anew: I will never know for sure.

After thirty years *(locked-in)* was *she* what I see before me
on the stage: old women in day-coats shuffling past rows of beds and
    sinks

the voices singing, not theirs, but singers standing in the orchestra's
   pit

—disembodied, so I can't locate the song in the singer.
I see the sacrificed carried away, elsewhere, off set.

24

She is the light of my mind as I yield to the sea beneath
a two-birded sky of a cloud-shredding evening.

This same teeming substance I've just learned to swim
in turns ominous when its translucence goes dim.

A vague glow of plankton reminds as it begins,
though I can't envision the face of my origin: once

she lived. It's this magical thinking I will to believe
as the summons of weightlessness lures me

to drift. The first star appears in the sky and I think:
others will follow, this thin abalone glare will be lit.

She is the pull of the moon, the slide of the tow.
She holds me in the water with the arms of a ghost.

When she ended her life, she took up in mine,
a street-dwelling squatter with nowhere to go.

She is not of the stars nor the sea nor the sky,
she is free of the myths she left with her life.

She glides in the night on the foam of a grave
—far from existence, she is Venus on the wave.

25

When the skin across the pond is settled
when the air is still, whatever is reflected shows clear.
Come to its edge. In the day the sky maybe blue
maybe gray around my shadow or my face

—maybe a Lotus flower (*preferring stagnant water*)
risen in the dawn half-opening each slim petal to the sun
or nothing more than my image beneath the sky.
In the night, if it is blessed or cursed I look

through dilated eyes and dare myself—will myself—
to see the half-closed face drowned in darkness searching
for a grace to re-establish a beginning in which
my appearance does no harm to my origin.

This is what love means for me:

to be missed before you depart
to be dreamed before you're seen—

a necessity and a vision.

26

I never asked to be saved from what I could not imagine.
My imagination is ever late to find the means it needs.

I thought I could do it: body you forth
create/make a formal being shapely enough

to restore you to some life, some will, some force—
Each October is the same. The cold is coming,

the leaves brown and drop to the ground.
They're brushed into mounds. They're set on fire—

Winter will arrive, and snow and morning frost and ice.
Nothing I imagine will (not) bring you forth or give you life.

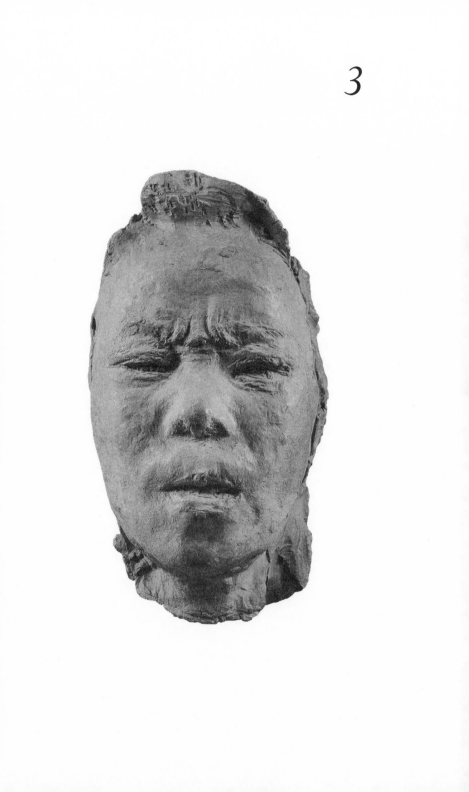

3

Primordial Subjects

1. INDEFINITE

The word *motherless* was never used
to describe who I am.

Your mother died, we separated early in your life,
she can't be found,

was never spoken. She simply never was.
I am minus one.

My father joked, *You were born from my head—*
A little goddess—

My child-mind is afraid. She wants to be
a girl, not ghost

not goddess. She wanders away to rhyme
"Do you like green eggs and ham?

Do you like them, Girl I am?" Don't you
have a mother?

"No, I come from something other."

2 . RELATIVE

I am nine months old. My brothers are older:
they can be raised without a mother.

I, an infant girl, I am given
to my grandmother and my eldest uncle's family.

My hair grows long and is braided each day
by female hands. I am groomed.

I belong to them, to then.
The domesticity of that life is a morning I lengthen

inside. In the opening of such light I speak
a language I forgot. I dream in it still, but when I rise

sound surrenders meaning. The syllables burn
that forest of symbols to the ground.

3 . PRONOUN

In my grandmother's
house, house of my once-family,
I found an old gilt photo

album hidden in the linen
brought from Korea. I wasn't
snooping, I loved the smell trapped

there. It smelled like trees
in winter. I sat
on the landing of the stairs, opening

the album when my cousin appeared.
There, on the page was my father—
not the blindingly beautiful young man

he was, but his emaciated twin
wearing glasses that didn't look like they belonged
on him. A woman stood

beside him, a woman I'd never seen.
Her face terrified me. She was pregnant
pearled and elegant in a red suit.

Her hair was combed smooth and held
back by a silk scarf. I wanted to look
away from *that face* without being seen.

My cousin asked, "Isn't she pretty?
Don't you know who she is?"
Blood rushed to my head.

I felt as if something, maybe I, would crack
wide open and spill glowy red across the old album
onto the bisque carpet. I was afraid

I would leave a stain, but I couldn't
look away. To my relief, no incision was made.
"That's your mother," my cousin said.

—*No*, I insisted, *That's Eartha Kitt*,
whose face had never before scared me
until now and still unless she's singing

There's one thing I really do need . . .
My cousin laughed. "No, she's black.
This is your mother."

"My father has pictures of their wedding.
He was there." *Where? Whose
wedding?* "Your parents. Your Mom-and-Dad's."

I don't have a mother. I don't
have a mother—and by magic, there she was:
standing beside my hollowed

father, head tilted, looking deep into my face
with her stiff, polished gaze. She looked
like a mask, she looked like my skin:

forebodingly strange, then utterly native.
She looked like a savage, now a dream.
Winnicott says the opposite of play in a child isn't work.

The opposing force to play in a child is reality.

4 . MOVABLE IDENTIFIERS

Once I saw the figure of my mother,
her face, I could no longer imagine

I was immune to biology. No longer
was I a *girl-thing*, I was a girl-

human? What did that mean?
How could I get myself out of this girl-

dwelling, back into a movable
thing, receding from killing sensations?

Disassociation is a mercy and skill, close
in kind to a magic spell, carrying the believer to

a divided realm of experience,
some distance from what compels it. In such an orbit,

the senses float, policing
whatever exceeds its limits. It takes more than will

to finesse the crossing from consciousness to the heavenly
relief of being bodiless. There, whatever harms does not

hurt, whatever fails to love or loves cannot be felt.
The penalty is severe. There is no paradise without a body.

The heavens we can trace are pleasures we make.
The crossing into being bodiless is total—

Little Girl's Auricle

I would swear this never happened.
I would know if it did, I would have remembered it.
If it did happen, I simply wasn't there, wasn't present for it.
But there I am, my bare tiny shoulders, my over-large head
resting on the rim of the tub, one finger in my mouth,
eyes wide and looking up.

He is so thin.
His bones poke out against his skin.

His shoulders curl into the head he is washing,
my brother's head, straining on his neck to stay still
as our father scrubs his hair and scalp clean.
This child is his favorite, the easiest to love, and is.
There is no evidence in the image, but I think beneath
the hands and suds, this brother is laughing, even if our father isn't.
Our father is deep in concentration, scrubbing his son clean. I imagine
I was next. I'd get into the bathwater when my brother was finished.
There is no image of this. The hunch of my father's back
over my head would confess the grief of love, the sorrow of his beast,
The enormous tragedy of the dream . . .

This, I've seen. I see it always. I carry it
in my torso as surely as a Buddhist lives in the skin of his own corpse.
In this photo, the blades of my father's bones lift
him and the one he cleans out of that bath, into the enterprise
of American life. I remember their flight—with one hand
waving goodbye—with the other I hid my eyes.
If he looked back, if he saw me, darkening
by his ascending light, surely I would not survive.

As he rose he burned clean
the Orpheus in him.

Carnal Incarnate

If I could rise from my body and leave it
behind in the bed where I try to sleep, I think

I might. This body has formed around
what it holds too tight from inside—hyper-

trophy in my pelvic muscles tilts my spine. The center
of mass of my body is askew. I lean slightly forward

always pushed ahead before I mean to proceed. It hurts
to be entered without tilting up or turning over. My lust, plotted

by relentless vigilance. When I am lover, I am
forever off angle. I want only to stare and not feel—

to be invisible to all I know to fear,
alive and far away from any body—not holy, just here.

The Muse (1907)

Wishing to obey
I hold my face in *The Anguish of Death*
for wounding lengths as his fingers knead,
pinch, press my gaze into clay.

For one mask he scooped out my eyes sixty-six times.
"Fatiguée!" I cried. My next death, he sanctified.

He claims I distill the spirit of death
with no willed innocence.
Coaxing me to hold heaven aside,
he commands my eyes wide—demands,
"You must not be pried from life before you die."

This alone lights him, lifts him.
He calls me his *divine faun*—
his *belle brilliante*: I sparkle, shine, yet
I must not rest my eyes.

In his merciless hands
we shift our shapes, leave our bodies
behind, we are pure spirit: lustral

lewd with life, *supernaturally alive—*
unless I tire. "Attends, Hanako!"
I falter and he is cursed.

Fully vacant, I wait where I posed.
He places natural lights around his finished mold.
My eyes at rest, radiance winks in me as a pulse.

I bring honor to the line.
I defy prohibition: as woman
I enact a warrior's sacrifice.

Mme. Rodin enters.
To greet her, I rise.
I begin my bow, I open my eyes.
Wavering knocks me to the ground.

What was inside is out.

A wreath of candles dances in-
candescence around the eyes of wished-for
ancestors. I am the *Head of Death*, his *palace of life*.

In the forty-first year of the Meiji
he gave me the Head of a martyr—
sainted, signified.

Trust

This is my calm world: sesame and soy and fat golden melon—
This world is glazed celadon, blues, grays, olives and clay.
The day starts slow and early. Crickets turn to birdsong at dawn.

The pink light of the new sun dissolves into smog.
The song never stops. The males sing, the females cry.

I wake in the bed where my grandmother dreamed and died.
I thought it was true: I was theirs—

We are yours. This, ours.

A childhood lies
where and when it survives. At five
I was told the arrangement was temporary.

I am your father.
These are your brothers.
This is a pet, a dog.

My world, whole—was gone.
All that was left: in my mouth alone.
No one spoke what I spoke.
My father thought it bad for my education.

This is where you were born, where you belong.

Yet here, back in this bed, rising
with the sun, I feel something
return to me. I wish to stay
in this revenant mundane: slow
rituals repeated day in-
to night, night into day.

Alias atque Alias

I dream a face
at night   Hazy
low and squatting

I wonder why
you will not
meet my gaze

In the day
I close my eyes
a face looks in-

to where I am
from where
you are fifty years away

I am not yet
born—still
to be conceived in

the mind, the body
beneath
The face

I see I have
never seen   It
was changed   erased

The eyes I seek
have never been
in my memory

no store-
house there
but hoarded here

frame by frame
Your face is then   is
thin   I thicken it

Thick Description

I cut lines of ink as I read through the night.
I imagine the margins on pages are slim wings
between plankton and stars. I find what I need
in far sources. I make them intimate,

I make them mine with the speed of light.

He was seventeen, just a man, still a boy and ready to die.
A true sacrifice, a living encounter—

                                   This father has paid
the sum of a daughter's dowry for his son to be consecrated
with a rod through his cheeks and tongue. The boy's face,
his mouth pierced and gaping, hangs on the page, helpless.

His clove-jelly eyes float and metamorphose into my mother's
eyes, eyes I can't possibly remember without images like his—
images forbidden, seized and smuggled into my life.
I can make anything mean what I need to find.

The stolen scrap, the plosive glance saturated in
longing is not looking at me: I am looking at *it*.

Every description is thick with a will to revivify—
reclaim, renounce, rename what is sought.

Blind hunger drives when I read. *A scream, the echo of*
a scream, hangs over that Nova Scotian village . . . and bit
by bit a village I've never seen swells into me. The ovoid
mouth of my mother's life, its slivering silence exists

in that scream—*unheard, in memory.* She came alive
forever—not loud, just alive forever redeemed from her never
with no speech. A noun transformed to modify
action revived her, returned her to me.

The words as they lay may refuse to say what you need.
Drop to your knees. Crawl beneath the overhanging,
the dangling down. Stroke the described,
from underneath. It reeks of the atavistic

to live. It survives by swallowing.

Screen Memories

The child moving on
this screen is unbearable.
She stands away
from the rushing stream. She turns her face

from the camera's lens. She weeps.
She hides one eye
with one hand—with the other,
she pats herself on her torso, soft and slow.

She wipes her tears
with the tips of her fingers. She is trying
to understand where she is. You can see
her in the corner of the frame

when the camera isn't aimed
at her. She watches
the scene from the top left edge,
from the sky, a ceiling.

*

When my husband's mother was dying
in days, maybe hours, I asked her,
"Is there anywhere special you'd like to go to die?"

"Here's fine," she replied. Excruciated—
out of fight. The tiny child in the home movie
seems to reply to the metaphysical

question that furrows her eyes
with the same answer as the wanting to die. *Eleanor,
child, where do you want to be?*

Here's fine—

*

I didn't yet speak English.
No one spoke Korean to me (though I tried).
For some time I had no language—
no language spoke for me, of me, to me.

My experience didn't mean anything to anyone.

My limbic system became my way to know.
How I felt became what I knew. This persists—
I feel before knowing, often the two are fused.
Sometimes knowing never arrives, but feeling?—

feeling rolls on, it pushes into me with no mercy.
It can take some time to unweave
what I feel from what I know and why and how.
I am forever late to experience.

The past is never exactly as I left it,
a different me remembers.
A different me seeks changing
pieces from the pile-up of feeling.

There is often a gap, a gape,
a lack of concordance that leaves me
feeling messy of mind, discordant,
out of control and angry. It leaves me feeling

left in another world not actually world—
suspended in the waiting to arrive.
I feel apart from others in this other world,
abandoned out there—in here:

this is the child I see on the screen.

*

I force myself to watch her again.
I hide my face with both hands.
I curl my legs into my torso.
I cannot get small enough.
I am still visible.

The sun is shining on the father.
He lifts the diminishing girl into the air.
The camera pans in close. The face,
my face, is larger than my two hands.
My eyes are as closed as I can make them.
Tears collect and fall from my chin.
The camera is ruthless. It does not flinch.

*

The father is shaking the sad girl
into the camera's lens. I am dizzy.
That child does not quite exist for her father.
She is held up as if she is pleasure prey,

a morbid trophy. What do I signify
for the screen-father? I press pause.
I zoom in as if the pixels, split apart, might
reveal meaning to me.

This child is decades away on a screen.
I can press stop. I can press eject. I can delete
forever, but I can't. I cannot un-see
this child. She is here in a now that never ends.

That child is creepy to me.
The gestures of comfort she performs
on her body are too old for her. In a scary movie
this child would be a serial killer or a ghost.

*

For a full year of my younger life
when the wound began I had no language,

no words to shape my experience.
Saying melted in my mouth, turned gummy.

The vacating of the only language I knew
stripped the smallest child-me of a vital organ: psychic

skin. Moderation of feeling. Meaning. The desertion,
the evacuation of my native tongue left me raw.

That bone-child grew a membrane, a neo-natal covering
as I absorbed English. It is too soft for touch.

I keep the bone-child small enough to survive without
words, tough enough to survive skinless.

She lives a life in me, closer to ghost,
to phantom or fairy. She is no child.

*

I have to write myself in
to make my way out of the
tiny child on the screen.

I hate that child. I don't want her
in me. I must get hard inside
to silence the life out of her.

Why did she stand there and watch?
Why didn't she scream? She should have
screamed in any voice she had,

even if no one could hear it.
She should have tried.
She should have spit it out

so it wouldn't grow so wild
within her. Kill her. Kill her.
Make the split clean as fire

blowing through her. Throw her
pieces into that stream.
Let the stream carry her into the river,

the river into the ocean.
Let the ocean disappear her
from the earth as if she never existed.

She almost didn't, but there
she stands. There I am
turning my face

away from the camera's lens—
the moving image keeps me
in a present tense.

Ghost in the Girl

His mother was taken before he accepted he wouldn't want her with the same bewildering force forever and ever. She disappeared before his love could be modified through the canons of kinship, rehearsed separations, objects of devotion, cathexis. He never learned. His mother's last birth was a girl. Together, they were taken and in a monstrous gesture: the infant returned a long-haired girl. The mother, censored—

    as if all trace of her could be erased,
    as if the void could be etched over,
    as if he could live safely on the earth with others, imaginary

firstborn, without her—*throbbing blankness, human palimpsest.*

Wound

You do not heal, you will not.
Made so long ago, you remain hidden

in extenso

high in contours I cannot see,
I cannot reach, but feel.

You let loose a fragment of scar
tissue, cells of his disorder.

Long ago, when this body was small
enough to rule he drew you again

and again. Endless lacerations, severance
forever fresh, dropping poppies

full-bloomed. He made you, wound
darkly hidden, you resume

forever, you heavy my center: un-wilting.
I see the red. I hear in red. In me, you are pure.

Theater of Ideas, New York (1907)

THE JAPANESE DUSE

I step into a wired costume—sparrow-sized
electric bulbs attach to its seams. They squeak
as I fasten in. A sinewy cord links me to a power
source taped beneath my navel. It is not umbilical.

It hangs between my legs: a snake gone flaccid.
From my basque, a hum as the stage goes black.
Ambient illumination is extinguished with a thump.
Its absence disturbs the audience. They murmur,

"Where is Little Hanako?" —That name they call is my lure.

I am seen across the stage as a constellation, sped.
Within its margin I brighten an ancient
dance drawn in a lucent pen. Small birds of light
pierce the dark with a ritual suicide.

Inside the sacrifice, I am neither woman nor man:
I am a drive to death—

open-eyed. I divine a sacred rite. White
viewers think this act savage. Their lust breathes
where they sit. As blade crosses belly a sack of fluid breaks a red
stain through heavy cloth, discharging what they cannot live

in the light. This "gruesome" act wrings
their muscles, moistens them. I am but a path—a figure
of dying, as when his fingers pressed my masticating
jaw, pinched my sideways eye looking into the other.

The Papers labeled me a Miniature, a Duse,
a Grotesque. Some bathed in their rage, exuberant
at my dance. I am long dead, but I survive. I am Rodin's
Head of Death, *Head of Sorrow*, "supernaturally alive."

Country-Child of War

My father's face is engraved with magic
ink: something other than its planes is promised.
After dinner, after forty years of silence he describes—
no, *re-experiences* his confusion in marrying
the stunning girl, an artist, an heiress (what luck!)
only to discover *she was not quite right*—
When I ask him why, how he knew it, he looks
deep into my eyes full of fear. It hurts my heart.
My father, whose inescapable beauty stuns me
still, is finally a country-child of war, devising
strategies to survive. Always afraid: he's ripe to be
tricked if he's not on guard. Tonight, he sits open:
young bridegroom to sheltered bride, afraid of her
family's wealth almost equal to its ignorance—

confused by who she was, what they together
made only to be unmade, undone by mystery, illness,
persistent threat that remains etched in his face
as he sits at four decades and half a world of distance.
"Great whales sing like birds. Their songs do not pass out
of the water into the air ... Modern technology transfers

these songs so we can hear them with our human ears."
He could do it—step into the sprawl of his
memory for answers to my questions, yet he is
my substratum: I go where he is taken. My need
to know my origin is the weight of a fixed star in him.
The balance of his inward drive to silence and my need
to pry my story out into the open keeps us torqued in
love: conjoined and struggling.

Head of Sorrow, Study of Hanako

The half-made head doesn't make sense.
The eyes are deranged and grotesque yet the cheeks
are full, her face furious with life.

It would be easy to mistake this clay as a mere study, given
the visible fingers of the maker across the brow,
the *being-made* degradation of the jaw, but these

inchoate traces make the face surge with life
in the being pulled apart in time. Beneath the surface
planes, action ends future act: time is stopped

in the instant it plays. Here is the instant of death,
as if I hear: Now it is safe to look at what was hidden
all your life. Such prohibitions terrify.

Was I afraid of what I might see, or was I afraid
to look? There is a gap, a black hole between the two.
I drop into that dark when I step.

Was she actually frightening, or was she scary
because she was unspeakable, broken,
fringe and the beginning of me?

How does the earthenware head make my hand rise?
Why do my fingers knead? Where do
I strain to touch? What did I learn was love?

Insulin

The treatment begins.
Hunger lashes her
body with its heavy whip.

The ether she breathes:
a field of blight dropping
a net far and wide to catch

the wet balls of her
eyes before they roll under
the tow of sugar's

rising wave as it crests then
crashes on the sand of her
foaming face.

Havoc

What remains of her: a havoc of antlers
—decades of insulin-shock coma leaving her
past the point of a body's tolerance.

Instead of counting sheep
she untangles a bramble of antlers, hidden
in the hut behind the nearest temple.

One step in, a sharp edge scrapes her shin.
She absorbs the sting while feeling
with her finger and toes for balance.

She cannot simply exert her will.
She must lift and cajole from within,
but how to get there? Ventriloquist? Mime?

The severed branching antlers
resemble one mass brain struck by lightning
or an atmospheric disturbance—

in order to extract one from the others
she must find her way inside the labyrinth;
pulling from the margin tightens the knot.

Each effort into the interior leaves
a trace on her body. Bruise, cut, laceration—
gash until she is razed and as far in as she can be.

Resting to catch her breath, she swallows
the stench of buck and blood. It makes her dizzy,
like musk. She remembers

she's there to undo the antlers, to sleep—
but she finds she cannot move. Her eyes
do not open to close or blink.

Call to Morning

In the portrayal of a grief-crazed woman in Noh, the process of
derangement is the plot's occasion. The mother is never permitted
to rejoin her lost child. A reunion of mother and child at the end
is not allowed, making it the most disconsolate of tragedies.

Cambridge. Snow falling fast and white and fat.
The streets outside merged, vanishing
to one vast plain of crystalline light.

You are on the way, said the mother
to the daughter through the poet
re-aligning Persephone/Demeter.

Terror of mother-love, daughter
—rape, rage at what separated
a mother from the Likeness she made.

My part read *I am waiting*—
I rose from my nursing daughter.
I asked, What am I waiting for?

What whiteness will you add to this whiteness,
                              what candor?
There will be no blanker whiteness than tonight is.
                              Find her.

She loved me once when the world was
asleep on a glowing white night like this. I have the image.
It shows my infant form in her arms . . . silken

robe, night, her profile pouring down into my waking face.
A daughter finds her mother after years of
months of days, decades away.

                              *

Late, so late that night
I call to morning, where she waits.
The phone rings, bells
in Ward 8, where no human race remains.

"Do you know who I am?"
I am Eleanor's mother. "Yes, Umma.
I am on my way."

Why did you wait?

*

Is there a scientific term for a death
that waits patiently in a body?

Removed from the three she made,
citizenry, the sane; how did she remain?

"Nature, when vital needs are at stake,
can erase the whole inner life."

*

You are on the way?
What does that correct?

Since I made you, you may

        imagine I set myself on fire—
        or better, say: you lit the funeral pyre
        from ten thousand days away.

Call It Love

I longed for your hair all day.
I missed being near as you lay under
the pain of a breathing machine. I wonder,

after this—elsewhere, what does remain of us?
What will become of the *we* we will always be?
What does your death mean for my *I*?

Do *we* cease with you? Do *we* die with your *are* and still
am and *is*? Will *we* derange by tones of tense as in *was*
and *wasn't* she waiting all this time, impossibly surviving

the decades it took to reunite?

*

My oldest friend, my fire-horse
beauty who fills big screens with her runic irony
meditates through smoky rings to soothe me.

Maybe death is cast with twin souls.
She asks me to imagine a womb weaves two souls,
one body: both grow, form and formless—

the formless existing always in
an altogether elsewhere after-birth. When the Earth-
ward is done, the soul of cells rejoins its primordial

whole in a purely other realm.
She's lived years in Los Angeles, you understand.
Still—is that what is happening in my absence?

*

Are you evaporating toward some *thing* transparent,
stirring, shapeless? Like the tiny pellucid foot that
"quite literally popped out like a breech birth"

from the brain tumor of a baby named Sam.
(Other parts, a thigh, a hand, were also found inside the tumor.)
A fetus in fetu occurs when one twin engulfs

the other in the womb. The engulfed
twin feeds off the other, is fatal if not removed. I read this
as a trope, a synecdoche; one part, say

a foot, for the whole of your formless other
engulfing you, erasing you, taking *you*, taking *matter*
into its own limpid hands

saying without syntax
the living can understand, *I miss you. Return to ME.*
I was there, I was your beginning, I am now your end.

You are my beginning. Your brain is dead.
Form gulping after formlessness, let go the air—
free soul from dust—*call it love.*

The Dream

Beneath the space of the stars
she was guided by the moon's instrument
from far away she was tossed in its great wave
making weightless the grave strain spread
inside her: sequela that confined her.

She is dead when I sleep, yet there
she swims. In the water by stroking arms
she escapes what she has lived. Bunraku
puppet turned real child withdrawing
limbs from the ninja's arms that mean

to guide her. It's not even a dream, I know—
the loss to which I wake: the lack of her breathing
face glowing there in the bay of an inland sea
elated to be floating weightless, looking
Heavenward and at me, but it is the dream I wish

to dream—my Origin, my life's mystery.
Gleam goodbye in my sleep under the last moon
before you die: your face all smooth, lit
white—peeled onion: *bob, cut tears
from my eyes. Wave and wink. A satellite. A spy.*

The Death

Your mother is dead.
"She choked on her morning egg."
They offered to keep her alive by machine
until I could arrange a trip to "encounter
the body before her death."

When insulin coma brought on by Insulin Shock
Treatment extends more than a *little*
past the limits of tolerance, deep coma will set in.
When the coma is too profound, pathological,
irrational reflexes will appear
in the place of normal nervous reflexes.

To see your mother's body,
How soon can you come?

Not soon enough.
Let her go, it is done.

She is an encumbrance in the field of activities of the living.
She cannot feel pain. She cannot feel anything.
She can stay this way for some time.

What is that cord hanging from her mouth?
Hyper-salivation, a corollary of the vagal
stimulation and areflexia.

The saliva becomes much thicker.
More viscous than normal, it can thicken
to the width of a garden
snake squeezing through the throat.

Abandon of the Eyes

It started early. Her missing
pearl choker, her ink brushes, her night
clothes, all disappeared

when she did. I imagine them where
she is, in a ruthless version of St. Augustine's
storehouse for memory, a *spreading*

limitless room for the hoarded
—a camp at a border holding hostage
all I have forgotten. I collect

proximities, imitations—agitating
totems—lavish, refugee
languages for love. I hoard

what I can. I lose by accumulation.
Such things take shape in my mind—
forgotten, but active: animated

by a devolution. I lift, keep, accrue all
I can find to escape, in that instant of
finding, an endless oil of wanting.

Head of Little Flowers

One day, I will walk immaculate
gardens to find you, there. With offerings
for the ancient deer, I will touch your eyelids,

your neck, the nest that was your hair.
I will rake your remains for bits of endocrine—
your palatine, a talus, an iliac wing.

All this is wish.

The dying die as they live,
not as pliable things—lithely addressed,
poured like glass into a *Head of Death.*

You died alone, as if we never spoke.
Among your "Beloved Remains," two silken
kerchiefs knotted into sacks carrying

paper in bits with your writing across
every surface, writing in images and Japanese
script dated decade by decade, time of day

by time of day.
I still do not know what
they say.

* * *

Author's Note

The dedication ink painting is by the poet's mother.
The first image is a portrait of the poet's mother.
The last image is the last photograph of the poet's mother.